TITLE PROJECT
268500405910

COUNTDOWN TO SPACE

SPACE EMERGENCY
Astronauts in Danger

Michael D. Cole

Series Advisor:
John E. McLeaish
Chief, Public Information Office, retired,
NASA Johnson Space Center

Enslow Publishers, Inc.
40 Industrial Road   PO Box 38
Box 398   Aldershot
Berkeley Heights, NJ 07922   Hants GU12 6BP
USA   UK
http://www.enslow.com

TITLE PROJECT
268500405910

Copyright © 2000 by Enslow Publishers, Inc.

All rights reserved.

No part of this book may be reproduced by any means without the written permission of the publisher.

Library of Congress Cataloging-in-Publication Data

Cole, Michael D.
    Space emergency : astronauts in danger / Michael D. Cole.
       p. cm. — (Countdown to space)
    Includes bibliographical references and index.
    Summary: Describes emergencies that occurred during several space missions, including Apollo 13, Friendship 7, Gemini 8, and Mir.
    ISBN 0-7660-1307-3
    1. Astronautics—Safety measures Juvenile literature. [1. Astronautics. 2. Space vehicle accidents.] I. Title. II. Series.
TL867.C6523   2000
629.45' 0028'9—dc21   99-26855
                                                                 CIP

Printed in the United States of America

10 9 8 7 6 5 4 3 2 1

To Our Readers: All Internet addresses in this book were active and appropriate when we went to press. Any comments or suggestions can be sent by e-mail to Comments@enslow.com or to the address on the back cover.

Photo Credits: National Aeronautics and Space Administration

Cover Illustration: NASA (foreground); Raghvendra Sahai and John Trauger (JPL), the WFPC2 science team, NASA, and AURA/STScI (background).

Cover photo: The first International Space Station crew practices water survival skills in the Black Sea. The skills would be needed if their spacecraft landed in the water instead of on land.

CONTENTS

1 Danger in Space 5

2 John Glenn and Friendship 7 15

3 The Gemini 8 Emergency 25

4 Mir and the
New Space Station 34

Chapter Notes 42

Glossary 44

Further Reading 46

Index 47

A successful liftoff of Apollo 13 was only the beginning of what became a space emergency.

1

Danger in Space

"Okay, Houston, we've had a problem here," said astronaut Jack Swigert, command module pilot of *Apollo 13*.[1]

Swigert and his crewmates, Jim Lovell and Fred Haise, were more than two hundred thousand miles away from Earth on their mission to the Moon. Their spacecraft was the Apollo command module *Odyssey*. Connected to the command module was the lunar module, the four-legged spacecraft that would make the landing on the Moon while the command module orbited above. On the evening of April 13, 1970, the three astronauts suddenly found themselves in an emergency situation.

"This is Houston, say again please."

Space Emergency

"Houston, we've had a problem," repeated Jim Lovell, the mission commander.

Lovell, Haise, and Swigert had just heard a loud bang inside the command module, then immediately felt their spacecraft shudder around them. They had either been hit by a small meteor or an explosion had occurred aboard their spacecraft. Warning lights were lighting up the astronauts' display panels. One of the first things Lovell discovered was that the power was dropping in one of the ship's three fuel cells. Within moments, the fuel cell had no power at all.

"We've had a main B bus undervolt," Lovell told Mission Control.

"Roger. Main B undervolt," Mission Control replied. "Okay, stand by 13. We're looking at it."[2]

Because the interior of the command module seemed to be okay, all three astronauts suspected that the lunar module had been struck by a meteor. The meteor's impact, they believed, had sent the spacecraft shuddering, and had caused their electrical system readouts to go crazy.[3]

But they were wrong.

The astronauts did not yet know it, but an electrical malfunction had caused an explosion aboard *Apollo 13*. The explosion had ruptured one of the command module's three oxygen tanks. The oxygen was used with hydrogen within the command module's fuel cells. The reaction produced electrical power for the ship.

Danger in Space

The lives of the Apollo 13 *astronauts were in danger when an explosion damaged an onboard oxygen tank, such as the one pictured here.*

Without enough oxygen to react in the fuel cells, the electrical systems would fail. If the electrical systems were not working, the crew would be unable to control the spacecraft.

The oxygen was not used for the electrical systems alone. The three astronauts also needed the oxygen to breathe. They would never survive the trip home without it. If they ran out of oxygen, they would die.

The damage to the command module was done within a matter of seconds, but it took the astronauts several minutes to discover exactly what had happened.

Lovell floated up to look at his instruments in the command module again. He now discovered that both fuel cells 1 and 3 were dead. This left only one remaining fuel cell to power the command module. Lovell got his crewmates' attention and pointed to the readouts of the two dead fuel cells.

"If these are real," he said, "the landing's off."[4]

The three men knew that with the failure of two fuel

Space Emergency

cells, NASA would automatically cancel their mission to land on the Moon. Failure of the third fuel cell would leave the crew stranded in space, and NASA would never take such a risk.

Lovell was very disappointed. But he soon realized their problems were far worse than a canceled Moon landing. At that moment, Lovell discovered the oxygen problem. He was shocked to find that the quantity indicator light on oxygen tank 2 read zero. The tank was empty!

Seconds later he looked at the quantity indicator light for oxygen tank 1. It, too, was dropping. One oxygen tank was empty and another was leaking. Lovell

In the Mission Operations Control Room, astronaut Fred Haise is seen on screen during a television transmission from Apollo 13. NASA canceled the crew's Moon landing after two fuel cells failed.

Danger in Space

now saw that they were in serious danger. With only one good oxygen tank to operate in the one remaining fuel cell, the spacecraft was badly crippled. The chances for the astronauts to return home alive did not look good. A life-threatening adventure lay ahead for the crew of *Apollo 13*.

Fortunately the lunar module *Aquarius* was still in perfect condition. But it was equipped only to support two men for two days. The astronauts and Mission Control now had to find a way for it to support three men for four days. *Aquarius* would be of tremendous help in getting them back to Earth's orbit, but it could not take them home.

Aquarius, designed only for a landing on the airless Moon, had no heat shield. The astronauts could not reenter Earth's atmosphere in *Aquarius*. Only *Odyssey*, with its reentry heat shield, could get them home. For the rest of the trip, all possible electrical power in *Odyssey* had to be conserved so it could be used at the end of the mission during reentry.

Two things had to work in order for Lovell, Haise, and Swigert to survive. First, an engine burn by *Aquarius* on the dark side of the Moon had to be successful to head them back toward Earth. Second, there had to be enough power in *Odyssey* at the end of the mission for them to make a safe reentry through Earth's atmosphere. If either of these were unsuccessful, they would die.

Space Emergency

To conserve power aboard *Odyssey*, Jack Swigert got the spacecraft almost completely powered down. This left it dark and very cold. It was an uncomfortable place for the astronauts to be, but *Aquarius* could hold only two of them at a time. The three of them took turns staying in *Odyssey*.[5]

It took nearly another day for *Apollo 13* to reach the Moon. During that time, the people at Mission Control worked around the clock to calculate a whole new plan that would bring the two spacecraft home. Normally, only the command module returned to Earth. This time, the landing engine of the lunar module *Aquarius* had to make the engine burn. Its engine had to burn long enough to set both *Aquarius* and *Odyssey* on a path that would carry them back to Earth.

Apollo 13 completed its swing around the Moon, but the astronauts were still a long way from home. Lovell, Swigert, and Haise felt some relief, though, in knowing that they were finally heading back toward Earth.[6]

"From the sounds of all the work that is going on," said Haise from the lunar module, "this flight is probably a lot bigger test for the system on the ground than up here."

"Well everybody down here is 100 percent optimistic," the capsule communicator assured him. "Looks like we're on the top side of the whole thing now."[7]

But there were other problems for the astronauts and Mission Control to solve during the return trip.

Danger in Space

After a swing around the Moon, the crew of Apollo 13—*Fred Haise, John Swigert, and James Lovell—were glad to be turned toward home. However, the most dangerous part of the journey still lay ahead.*

Humans inhale oxygen and exhale carbon dioxide. Inside the two spacecraft, deadly amounts of carbon dioxide were building up. Too much carbon dioxide would kill the astronauts. One of the lunar module's odor canisters for carbon dioxide removal was taped tightly to the end of a hose to try to filter the carbon dioxide from the air. As air was sucked through the hose, the canister's filter trapped the carbon dioxide particles, making the air safer for the astronauts to breathe. It was a strange-looking creation, but it worked.

In an effort to conserve water, the astronauts had

Space Emergency

drunk very little since the crisis began. After three days, this lack of water had caused Fred Haise to become ill with a kidney infection. He could not control his shivering. The astronauts were almost home, but they were cold, hungry, thirsty, and exhausted.

By the morning of April 17, *Apollo 13* was only twenty thousand miles from Earth. The command module was once again powered up. Nearly four days had passed since the explosion, but everything seemed to be working. The service module section of the command module was let go from *Odyssey* in preparation for reentry. The astronauts watched out their windows as the service module section floated away. They could not believe what they saw.

"There's one whole side of that spacecraft missing!" Lovell said.

"Is that right!" the capcom answered.

"Right near the high-gain antenna, the whole panel is blown out, almost from the base to the engine."[8]

Later, *Aquarius* was also let go into space. The command module was now ready for reentry. The capsule slid into the atmosphere just as the people at Mission Control had planned. The reentry radio blackout lasted longer than the usual three minutes. After three and a-half minutes there was still no answer from *Apollo 13*. People at Mission Control began to fear that their best efforts to save the astronauts had not been enough.

Danger in Space

Then, after almost four minutes of reentry radio blackout, Swigert answered the calls from Mission Control. The three astronauts had survived reentry in *Odyssey*. They were okay! The parachutes deployed and the astronauts splashed down safely in the Pacific.

Apollo 13 had made it!

"There has never been a happier moment in the United States space program," NASA administrator

Capsule splashdown in the Pacific Ocean was NASA's happiest moment. Apollo 13 *had made it!*

Space Emergency

Thomas Paine said later. "Although the *Apollo 13* mission must be recorded as a failure, there has never been a more prideful moment."[9]

Apollo 13 was the closest NASA had ever come to losing a crew of astronauts in space. Through a tremendous effort by everyone involved with the mission and the space program, the three astronauts made it home.

Apollo 13 had not been NASA's first space mission to experience problems. Emergencies in space began with the very first American to orbit Earth.

2

John Glenn and Friendship 7

John Glenn waited for the final seconds of the countdown to tick away.

The date was February 20, 1962. Glenn was at the controls of his small Mercury capsule, *Friendship 7*, atop a powerful Atlas rocket poised upon the launchpad. If all went well with his mission, he would become the first American to orbit Earth.

His friend and fellow astronaut Scott Carpenter communicated with him by radio from the blockhouse not far from the launchpad. Two other American astronauts had gone successfully into space already, but this would be the first attempt at an orbital flight around Earth. It was a dangerous business, and everyone involved with the flight knew it.

Space Emergency

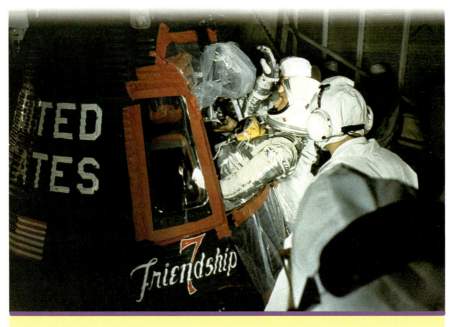

On February 20, 1962, John Glenn was helped into the Friendship 7 *capsule. He was about to attempt America's first orbit of Earth.*

John Glenn was risking his life on this mission. Now it was about to begin.

"Godspeed, John Glenn," Carpenter said. "Ten, nine, eight, seven, six, five, four . . . three . . . two . . . one. Zero!"[1]

The mighty engines rumbled beneath Glenn. A moment later he felt the rocket surge upward off the pad. "Liftoff!" he heard in his space helmet's headset.

"Roger," Glenn answered excitedly. The special mission clock on his instrument panel began to count the time. "The clock is operating! We're underway!"[2]

Glenn and *Friendship 7* roared into the sky, going

John Glenn and Friendship 7

faster and faster as the rocket climbed toward space. Within minutes the spacecraft had reached the incredible speed of 17,500 miles per hour, and the rocket separated from *Friendship 7*.

John Glenn was successfully in orbit, alone in the *Friendship 7* capsule.

He was scheduled to make three orbits on his mission. The flight went perfectly through most of the first orbit. It took *Friendship 7* about ninety minutes to go around Earth. He experienced some trouble when a small thruster was pushing the capsule slightly out of its correct position. The automatic pilot would then correct it, but the whole process was wasting fuel Glenn would later need to keep *Friendship 7* in the correct position for reentry. To conserve fuel, Glenn switched off the automatic pilot and took manual control of the spacecraft.

But Glenn was unaware of a greater problem. Near the end of that first orbit, Mercury Control noticed a disturbing signal coming from the capsule. The signal indicated that the landing bag was loose. The landing bag was designed to spring out like a jack-in-the-box from the blunt end of the capsule near the end of the mission. As the capsule floated down on parachutes toward the ocean, the landing bag would help cushion the capsule's impact with the water.

If the landing bag had popped out while Glenn was still in orbit, the heat shield covering the blunt end of

Space Emergency

the capsule would also have come loose from the rest of the spacecraft. Without the heat shield securely in place, *Friendship 7* would burn up like a meteor when it reentered the atmosphere. John Glenn would surely die.

Mercury Control did not want to concern Glenn with the trouble until they knew exactly what they wanted him to do about it. A set of rockets called the retropackage were attached on top of the heat shield by three metal straps. Normally the straps were cut loose before reentry began, releasing the retropackage and exposing the heat shield to the heat of reentry. Mercury Control believed that if these straps were kept on, they would hold the heat shield safely in place until reentry.

Capsule communicators, or capcoms as they were called, were stationed around the globe to communicate with Glenn as he orbited. One of the them, stationed in Australia, was Glenn's fellow astronaut Gordon Cooper. Cooper was the first to ask about the problem.

"Will you confirm the

From inside his cramped capsule, John Glenn talks with Mercury Control.

John Glenn and Friendship 7

Landing Bag switch is in the off position? Over," Cooper asked.[3]

"That is affirmative," Glenn said. "Landing Bag switch is in the center off position." Later, the capcom at the Canton Island station hinted at the confusion and concern they were experiencing over the landing bag situation.

"We also have no indication that your landing bag might be deployed," he said.

"Did someone report landing bag could be down?" Glenn asked. The capcom denied that there was any problem. But by that time Mercury Control was considering whether to go ahead with the third orbit or bring Glenn down.

"Do you still consider yourself 'GO' for the next orbit?" the capcom in Hawaii asked.

"That is affirmative," Glenn said. "I am 'GO' for the next orbit."

For the third time, Glenn and *Friendship 7* orbited high above the Atlantic Ocean, Africa, Australia, and then the Pacific Ocean. As he neared Hawaii again, it was time to prepare for reentry. Mercury Control then informed him of the possible problem with the heat shield.

"We have been reading an indication on the ground of segment 51, which is Landing Bag Deploy," the Hawaii capcom said. "Cape [Flight] would like you to check this by putting the landing bag switch in auto

Space Emergency

position, and see if you get a light [to indicate the landing bag had deployed]. Do you concur with this? Over."

Glenn now realized the reason for all the questions about the landing bag. He knew this could be a serious problem. Mercury Control believed the signal might be an error. Yet now they wanted him to fool around with the switch. Glenn thought this was unwise. Messing with the landing bag switch might make it pop out if it had not done so already. Against his own judgment, he followed orders and flipped the switch.

There was no green light.

"Negative," Glenn said, "in automatic position did not get a light and I'm back in off position now. Over."

The heat shield appeared to be okay, but Mercury Control decided they could not take any chances. After the retropackage had fired and normal gravity settled over Glenn once again, he was told to leave the retropackage on through the entire reentry. But he was not told why. Glenn believed it was time they told him what they knew.

"This is *Friendship 7*. What is the reason for this? Do you have any reason? Over."

"Not at this time," the Texas capcom told him. "This is the judgment of Cape Flight."

Finally, fellow astronaut Alan Shepard told him from Mercury Control, "We are not sure whether or not your landing bag has deployed. We feel it is possible to reenter

John Glenn and Friendship 7

Capcom Alan Shepard monitors Friendship 7 *from Mercury Control.*

with the retropackage on. We see no difficulty at this time with that type of reentry."

It had already started. Glenn was busy using his hand controller to keep the capsule at the proper angle for reentry. In a matter of minutes, all questions about the heat shield would be answered. Glenn's heart began beating faster. If the heat shield was loose, he would feel the heat against his back very soon.[4]

Glowing heat began to surround *Friendship 7* and started to interfere with the radio communications. As

Space Emergency

expected during this high-heat phase of reentry, Glenn began to lose contact with Mercury Control.

"Go ahead, Cape, you're OK ground, you are going out," he said.

A moment later, all radio signals were blocked by the barrier of ionized particles created by reentry heat. The capsule was rocking in every direction as Glenn struggled to control it. He saw flaming chunks fly past his window. He could not know for sure if they were chunks of the retropackage or the heat shield.[5]

"This is *Friendship 7*," Glenn said into his voice recorder. "A real fireball outside."

As Mercury Control waited through reentry, Alan Shepard nervously called over and over for Glenn to respond. "*Friendship 7*, this is Cape. Do you read? Seven, this is Cape. Do you read? Over."

Shepard continued to call Glenn, but there was no response. The people in the control room began to fear that John Glenn had been burned alive. "*Friendship 7*, this is Cape. Do you read? Over," Shepard called again. Then everyone heard a sudden crackling on the radio.

"Loud and clear; how me?" Glenn replied to everyone's great relief.

"Roger, reading you loud and clear," Shepard said. "How are you doing?"

"My condition is good," Glenn said, "but that was a real fireball, boy. I had great chunks of that retropack breaking off all the way through."

John Glenn and Friendship 7

Navy crews hook recovery equipment to Friendship 7 *as the spacecraft is hoisted from the ocean. The heat shield had worked, and John Glenn became an American hero.*

The heat shield had done its job. John Glenn had survived the bumpy and dangerous reentry. The parachutes soon sprung from the nose of the capsule, and *Friendship 7* floated safely to a splashdown in the Atlantic Ocean.

John Glenn, the first American to orbit Earth, became a national hero. Thirty-six years later, at the age of seventy-seven, Glenn made a second trip into space. After serving many years as a United States senator, Glenn orbited Earth once again as a crew member of the space shuttle *Discovery* in 1998.

"I got great satisfaction the first time out of just being up there and being the first one to do this for our country," Glenn said after his second flight. "And here I am all these years later. I am very, very proud and have a great sense of satisfaction of participating with such a great crew as this."[6]

Glenn always recognized the tremendous amount of teamwork required to make a spaceflight successful.

Space Emergency

Without the knowledge, intelligence, and skills of everyone involved in Project Mercury, Glenn might never have survived the flight of *Friendship 7*. Their talents, along with Glenn's own training and courage, brought this first space emergency to a happy end.

In 1998, John Glenn returned to space aboard the space shuttle Discovery. He became the oldest person to make a trip into space.

3

The Gemini 8 Emergency

There were six flights of the one-person Mercury spacecraft, including John Glenn's *Friendship 7* mission. The next manned space vehicle built by NASA was the two-person Gemini spacecraft.

Gemini looked very similar to the Mercury capsule. But the slightly larger Gemini was equipped with a set of rocket thrusters that could change its orbit. It also had hatches that swung open above the astronauts to let them out more easily. These hatches allowed space-suited astronauts to venture out of the spacecraft for some of the very first spacewalks.

The Gemini flights were designed to gain experience at the tasks of rendezvous and docking in space. Rendezvous occurs when two spacecraft come near each

Space Emergency

other. Docking occurs when they are linked, or connected. Those skills had to be learned before astronauts could make the trip to the Moon in the later Apollo program. *Gemini 8*'s mission was to go into orbit and dock with an unmanned Agena rocket, which had been launched earlier. The Agena served as the target vehicle for *Gemini 8*'s docking practice.

The crew of *Gemini 8* were astronauts David Scott and Neil Armstrong. Neither man had flown in space before. Their mission was to attempt the first docking ever of two spacecraft. Scott was also scheduled to make a two-hour spacewalk.[1]

Armstrong and Scott suited up at Cape Kennedy on the morning of March 16, 1966. As their physical condition and the operation of their space suits were checked, the Agena target vehicle lifted off from pad 14. The launch went perfectly and the Agena was

In the white room that led to the Gemini 8 *spacecraft, David Scott (left) and Neil Armstrong test their space suits. They were to attempt the first docking of two spacecraft.*

The Gemini 8 Emergency

soon in orbit. Later that morning the astronauts were driven to their own launchpad. Armstrong and Scott climbed into the cockpit of *Gemini 8* and checked their instruments as the countdown proceeded. At 11:41 A.M., the Titan rocket lifted *Gemini 8* off the pad and roared through the late morning clouds toward space. Within minutes Armstrong and Scott were in orbit.

During the first four orbits, the two astronauts fired a number of bursts from their rockets to move their spacecraft to a higher orbit. The bursts boosted them closer to the path of the Agena, which was orbiting at 185 miles above Earth. *Gemini 8* then made radar contact with the target. Nearly five hours after liftoff, the two astronauts looked out their windows and sighted the Agena.

With steady hands, Armstrong began the final maneuvers to bring *Gemini 8* within two feet of the Agena. Armstrong gently pressed his spacecraft forward until the Agena's docking adapter latched on to the nose of *Gemini 8*.

"Flight, we are docked," Armstrong said. "It was a real smoothie."[2]

The two spacecraft were now connected by the docking adapter and appeared to be very stable.

"OK, just for your information," Armstrong reported, "the Agena was very stable. And at the present time, we're having no noticeable oscillations at all."[3]

The connection in the adapter had also connected

Space Emergency

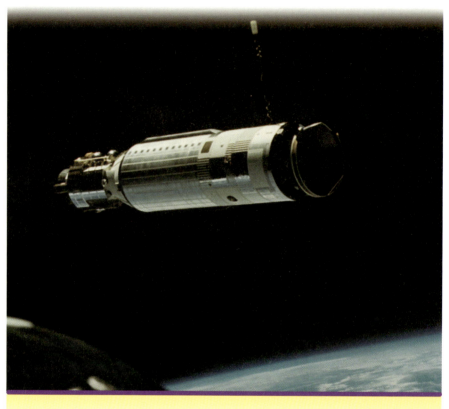

The Gemini 8 astronauts spotted the Agena from their windows.

Gemini 8 electronically to the Agena's thruster control system. The astronauts tested the Agena's thrusters by having it move the two spacecraft to a different angle. It seemed to work very smoothly. But a short time later, David Scott noticed they had begun to drift from their original position. Something was clearly pushing the two spacecraft.

Armstrong and Scott thought one of their thrusters might be stuck. But when they did not hear the usual

The Gemini 8 Emergency

hissing sound from their spacecraft's thrusters, they decided the problem had to be with the Agena.[4]

Armstrong used *Gemini 8*'s thrusters to try to steady the two spacecraft. His efforts worked for a short time. Then the Agena and *Gemini 8* began to tumble. They were soon spinning around at a rate of nearly twenty times a minute—once every three seconds. The spacecraft was also about to pass out of radio contact with the ground network for the next few minutes as the astronauts passed over the Pacific Ocean. With no help from Mission Control, Armstrong and Scott would have to try to solve the problem themselves.

Armstrong was afraid that if their rate of tumbling got any worse, it would break the docking assembly and damage *Gemini 8*. He decided he must undock the two spacecraft. Armstrong managed to slow the tumbling until he thought he could safely disengage from the Agena. At this point, both astronauts expected the Agena to go spinning out of control, while they quickly stabilized *Gemini 8*.

The Gemini capsule separated from the Agena. To the great surprise of Armstrong and Scott, *their* spacecraft began to tumble at a higher rate than ever. Both men quickly realized that it had been *Gemini 8* causing the problem all along. *Gemini 8* began to tumble end over end. Within moments the tumbling had built up to a dangerous rate of sixty revolutions per minute—once every second! Such a dizzying rate of tumble

Space Emergency

threatened to cause Armstrong and Scott to black out. When the control panels started blurring before their eyes, the astronauts' hearts began to race. Finally they came back into contact with the ground network.[5]

"We have a serious problem here," Armstrong reported. "We're tumbling end over end up here. We've disengaged from the Agena."[6]

Gripping the control handle, Armstrong tried every

David Scott trained for his space mission in a C-135 Air Force plane. This training proved necessary as he and Armstrong fought to keep consciousness aboard Gemini 8.

The Gemini 8 Emergency

possible maneuver to slow the tumbling. Nothing seemed to work.

"We're in violent left roll," Armstrong said. "We seem to have a stuck thruster."[7]

They were dangerously close to losing consciousness in the spinning capsule. Mission Control still struggled to figure out what was happening.

"Did he say he could not turn the Agena off?" asked one controller.

"No," replied another. "He said he's disengaged from the Agena! And he's in a roll, and he can't stop it!"[8]

The capsule continued to spin. None of Armstrong's efforts with the thrusters were working. It looked hopeless.

"We're rolling now because we can't turn anything off!" Scott told Mission Control. "We are increasing in a left roll!"[9]

Armstrong then made a desperate move to save himself and his crewmate. He activated the reentry thruster system. As the reentry thrusters fired, he used several bursts from the smaller thrusters to get the capsule back into a steady position. After ten very anxious minutes of crisis, Neil Armstrong brought *Gemini 8* back under control.

Armstrong's shrewd move to fire the reentry thrusters had saved them, but it had used 75 percent of the reentry thruster fuel. As a result of the fuel situation, they had to come down on the very next orbit.[10] Instead

Space Emergency

of coming down in the Atlantic, the emergency splashdown was now to occur in the Pacific Ocean near the island of Okinawa.

Reentry went perfectly with the remaining fuel, and the astronauts splashed down safely in the Pacific. They were recovered three hours later by a U.S. Navy destroyer. Scott had been unable to make his spacewalk,

The Gemini 8 *spacecraft, with Armstrong and Scott still aboard, is hoisted aboard the destroyer USS* Leonard Mason. *Although trouble with the maneuvering system forced NASA to end the mission early, the astronauts were safe.*

and the emergency had cut the mission short. But after coming dangerously close to dying in space, Neil Armstrong and David Scott were home safely.

"The flight crew and ground crew," said NASA's Dr. Robert Gilruth, "reacted extremely well and ably to an inflight emergency and we feel very fortunate to have experienced a problem like this and to have been able to overcome it and bring the craft back successfully."[11]

David Scott and Neil Armstrong had proved the effectiveness of their astronaut training during the emergency.

Spaceflight is still a dangerous operation, and the astronauts who travel in space today understand the risks of their job. Today astronauts from the United States, Russia, Japan, Canada, Germany, and other nations are working together in space. They are also experiencing space emergencies together.

4

Mir and the New Space Station

A space station is an orbiting laboratory in space. For a number of years, Russian cosmonauts and American astronauts worked together aboard the Russian *Mir* space station.

NASA astronaut Michael Foale was aboard *Mir* in 1997 when a Russian Progress resupply vehicle was about to dock with the station. He and his Russian crewmates, Vasili Tsibliyev and Alexander Lazutkin, were going to dock the vehicle manually. They were unable to use a guidance system they had previously used for such operations.

On June 25, 1997, Tsibliyev and Lazutkin were ready at the control panel in *Mir*'s core module. A camera mounted aboard Progress sent images of its movement

Mir and the New Space Station

On July 25, 1997, the Russian Mir space station was the site of another space emergency.

Space Emergency

toward *Mir* to the monitor beside Tsibliyev's controls. Tsibliyev watched the monitor and controlled Progress remotely with a set of joysticks. Lazutkin watched for the spacecraft's approach at a nearby window. Foale was ahead of them in another of the station's modules called the Kvant 1. The Progress vehicle was to dock with the Kvant 1 module. Foale was watching through a window for the vehicle to come down toward the Kvant 1 module from above.

Progress was several hundred yards away when they began the operation. Before long, Tsibliyev noticed that something was wrong. Progress was coming toward the station too fast. With the joysticks, he applied a braking thrust to the vehicle, but it was not stopping! In a few moments, the vehicle was within 150 feet of the station.

"There it is already!" Lazutkin shouted from his window. "It's coming in! Fast!"

Tsibliyev watched his monitor. He knew that Progress was going to hit the station.

"Michael! Get in the spacecraft!" he shouted to Foale.[1]

Docked to the station was a Soyuz spacecraft, which carried astronauts to the space station and back to Earth. Tsibliyev wanted Foale to power it up immediately in case they needed to use it to abandon the station. Foale headed for the Soyuz, as Commander Tsibliyev held onto the sticks to keep the Progress from hitting the core module.

36

Mir and the New Space Station

Inside Mir, the modules connect at this transfer node. The astronauts worked together to control the damage caused by the collision.

"If it had hit us directly," Tsibliyev said later, "it would have punctured the core module directly and we would have all died."[2]

Instead, the vehicle crashed into the Specktr science module. Lazutkin saw it. The three men felt their ears pop as air pressure began leaking from the station. If the air pressure leaked from the station too quickly for them to stop it, the astronauts would die from a lack of oxygen. Lazutkin immediately floated over to where Foale was disconnecting cables in preparation for sealing the hatch of the Soyuz. This was also the connecting point to the Spektr science module. The two of them worked together disconnecting the cables between the

Space Emergency

station and both the Soyuz and the Spektr module. A half hour later they sealed the hatch to the Spektr module, and the air pressure inside the station slowly went back to normal. But they were still in trouble.

The impact of the Progress vehicle had knocked the station into a slow roll. Without *Mir*'s solar panels angled continuously into the sun, the panels could not produce the electrical power needed to run the station. The crew's instrument panels went dark. Until the rolling motion was stopped and the solar panels were again aimed at the sun, they would be unable to control the station.

Ground controllers could fire *Mir*'s thrusters to stop the roll. The controllers, however, needed to know the rate of the roll in order to know how long to fire the thrusters. But without power to their instruments, *Mir*'s crew could not determine the rate of roll.

Astronaut Foale thought of something that might work.

At one of the station's windows, he held his thumb out at arm's length. Foale knew from backyard astronomy that his thumb held out this way blotted out a patch of sky equal to about one and a-half degrees of arc. Checking his watch, and following the stars as they disappeared and reappeared from behind his thumb, Foale obtained a close estimate of the rate at which the station was rolling.

Mir and the New Space Station

Astronaut Michael Foale used his knowledge of astronomy to help ground controllers take care of their spinning space station.

"Tell them we're moving one degree per second," Foale said.[3]

His estimate was radioed to the ground controllers. *Mir*'s thrusters were fired to stop the one-degree-per-second roll. Within moments the station stopped rolling. Sunlight hit the solar panels, and their instruments were soon working again.

The three space station crew members—two Russian, one American—had worked together to rescue themselves from an emergency situation in space.

Mir was an old space station when this and other smaller emergencies occurred aboard it. The station was

Space Emergency

operating far beyond what it had been designed for. NASA and other space agencies began construction of the International Space Station (ISS) in November 1998. ISS is much larger than *Mir* and is designed and built with the latest technology. Construction on the station is planned to continue through the year 2002.

So far the astronauts working aboard the station, and on its construction, have encountered no major emergencies. But this does not mean that accidents will never happen. The dangers of being in space can never be completely eliminated.

In a giant swimming pool, astronauts Jerry Ross and Jim Newman train for the spacewalks they will perform during assembly of the International Space Station. Their training will prepare them for possible emergencies.

Mir and the New Space Station

Scientists and engineers build the safest equipment possible for astronauts to use in space. These scientists and engineers do their best to prevent emergencies from occurring. Astronauts spend years training for their space missions. They use simulators to practice how they will deal with many kinds of emergencies that might occur while they are in space.

This kind of training saved the lives of John Glenn, Neil Armstrong, and David Scott. It taught the crew of *Apollo 13* the skills they would need to solve their many difficulties. It prepared the Russian and American astronauts aboard *Mir* for the unexpected dangers of life aboard the space station. Training, preparation, and the ability to think quickly and clearly are the astronauts' best tools for dealing with space emergencies.

CHAPTER NOTES

Chapter 1. Danger in Space

1. *Apollo 13, Technical Air-to-Ground Voice Transcription*, Manned Spacecraft Center, Houston, Texas, April 1970.

2. Richard S. Lewis, *The Voyages of Apollo* (New York: The New York Times Book Company, 1974), pp. 158–159.

3. Jim Lovell and Jeffrey Kluger, *Lost Moon: The Perilous Voyage of Apollo 13* (New York: Houghton Mifflin Company, 1994), pp. 96–97.

4. Ibid., p. 100.

5. Ibid., pp. 202–203.

6. Peter Bond, *Heroes in Space: From Gagarin to Challenger* (New York: Basil Blackwell Inc., 1987), p. 235.

7. David Baker, *The History of Manned Space Flight* (New York: Crown Publishers, 1982), p. 380.

8. Lewis, p. 168.

9. Bond, p. 241.

Chapter 2. John Glenn and Friendship 7

1. *To the Moon* (record documentary), Time/Life Records, 1970.

2. *Results of the First United States Manned Orbital Space Flight* (Washington, D.C.: National Aeronautics and Space Administration, 1962), p. 149.

3. Ibid., p. 171. (All in-flight communications that follow in this chapter come from this source.)

Chapter Notes

4. Personal interview with John Glenn, June 18, 1991.
5. "Spaceflight Part 2: The Wings of Mercury," narrated by Martin Sheen, PBS Video (1985).
6. Tom Diemer, "Sen. Glenn Readjusting to Being Earthbound," *Plain Dealer*, November 9, 1998, p. 1A.

Chapter 3. The Gemini 8 Emergency

1. Peter Bond, *Heroes in Space: From Gagarin to Challenger* (New York: Basil Blackwell Inc., 1987), pp. 111–112.
2. Ibid., p. 112.
3. "Spaceflight Part 2: The Wings of Mercury," narrated by Martin Sheen, PBS Video (1985).
4. Bond, pp. 112–113.
5. Alan Shepard and Deke Slayton, *Moon Shot: The Inside Story of America's Race to the Moon* (Atlanta: Turner Publishing, Inc. 1994), pp. 184–185.
6. Ibid., p. 185.
7. Bond, p. 113.
8. "Spaceflight, Part 2."
9. Ibid.
10. Shepard and Slayton, p. 185.
11. Bond, p. 114.

Chapter 4. Mir and the New Space Station

1. Jeffrey Kluger, "A Bad Day in Space," *Time*, November 3, 1997, p. 89.
2. Jim Banke, "Moscow, We Have a Problem," *Ad Astra*, September/October 1997, p. 33.
3. Kluger, p. 91.

GLOSSARY

blockhouse—A strong, thickly protected building near the launchpad where engineers and technicians monitor the launch.

capcom (capsule communicator)—The person who communicates directly with astronauts in the spacecraft; the capcom is usually another astronaut.

command module—The Apollo spacecraft that carried three astronauts into orbit around the Moon. It also carried the astronauts home through reentry into Earth's atmosphere.

docking—The connecting of two spacecraft in space.

engine burn—The action of firing a spacecraft's rocket engine for a specific period.

fuel cell—A device that uses elements, such as hydrogen and oxygen, to create a reaction that gives off energy to power a machine such as a spacecraft.

heat shield—The surface that covered the reentry side of early spacecraft. Parts of the surface were designed to burn away. This process carried heat away and prevented heat from building up on the spacecraft.

landing bag—The coiled-up cushion packed into the blunt end of the Mercury spacecraft. It was designed to soften the spacecraft's impact with the water at splashdown.

Glossary

lunar module—The Apollo spacecraft that landed astronauts on the Moon and brought them back up to meet with the command module.

meteor—A rock or piece of dust in space, which makes a streak of light when entering Earth's atmosphere.

NASA (National Aeronautics and Space Administration)—The United States government agency in charge of space activities.

reentry—The return through Earth's atmosphere.

rendezvous—The near meeting of two objects, such as two spacecraft in space.

retropackage—The rockets strapped to the blunt end of the Mercury spacecraft; these were fired to slow the spacecraft to prepare for reentry.

simulator—A machine or environment that allows astronauts to practice for their work in space. One computerized flight simulator allows astronauts to practice landing the shuttle. Another simulator, a large swimming pool, creates a feeling of weightlessness that allows astronauts to practice for their spacewalks.

solar array—Panels of silicon material that absorb the energy from the sun and transform it into electrical energy for spacecraft and other devices.

spacewalk—The act of putting on a space suit and leaving the pressurized cabin of a spacecraft to conduct activities outside the spacecraft.

thruster—A small rocket system used to control the position of a spacecraft in space.

trajectory—The given path of a moving object through space.

FURTHER READING

Books

Berliner, Don. *Living in Space.* Minneapolis, Minn.: The Lerner Publishing Group, 1993.

Bernards, Neal. *Mir Space Station.* Mankato: Minn.: The Creative Company, 1999.

Landau, Elaine. *Space Disasters.* New York: Franklin Watts, Inc., 1999.

Stott, Carole, ed. *Space Facts.* New York: DK Publishing, Inc., 1995.

Internet Addresses

Bray, Becky, and Patrick Meyer. "Kid's Space." March 27, 1998. <http://liftoff.msfc.nasa.gov/Kids> (March 23, 1999).

Data Matrix, Inc. "The Astronaut Connection." n.d. <http://nauts.com> (March 23, 1999).

McCracken, Pat. "NASA Office of Spaceflight." n.d. <http://www.hq.nasa.gov/osf> (March 23, 1999).

National Space Society. "Space Exploration Online." July 14, 1998. <http://www.ari.net/nss/seo/home.html> (March 23, 1999).

INDEX

A

Agena rocket, 26, 27, 28, 29, 30, 31
Apollo 13 mission, 5–15, 41
  command module, 5, 6, 7, 10, 12. See also *Odyssey*.
  explosion, 6–7, 12
  lunar module, 5, 6, 10, 11. See also *Aquarius*.
Aquarius, 9, 10, 12
Armstrong, Neil, 26, 27, 28–29, 30–31, 33, 41

C

Carpenter, Scott, 15, 16
Cooper, Gordon, 18–19

D

Discovery, 23

F

Foale, Michael, 34, 36, 37, 38–39
Friendship 7 mission, 15–23, 24
  landing bag, 17–18, 19–20

G

Gemini 8 mission, 26, 27–33
  tumbling, 29–31
Gemini program, 25–26
Gilruth, Robert, 33
Glenn, John, 15, 16–17, 18, 19, 20, 21, 22, 23, 24, 25, 41

H

Haise, Fred, 5, 6, 9, 10, 12

I

International Space Station (ISS), 40

K

Kvant 1, 36

L

Lazutkin, Alexander, 34, 36, 37
Lovell, James, 5, 6, 7, 8, 9, 10, 12

M

Mercury Control, 17, 18, 19, 20, 22, 29, 31
Mir, 34, 36–40, 41
  collision, 36–37
  tumble, 38

47

Mission Control, 6, 9, 10, 12, 13

N
NASA, 8, 13, 14, 25, 33, 40

O
Odyssey, 5, 9, 10, 12, 13

P
Paine, Thomas, 14
Progress, 34, 36, 38
Project Mercury, 24

S
Scott, David, 26, 27, 28–29, 30, 31, 32, 33, 41
Shepard, Alan, 20–21, 22
Soyuz, 36, 37, 38
Specktr science model, 37, 38
Swigert, Jack, 5, 6, 9, 10, 12, 13

T
Tsibliyev, Vasili, 34, 36, 37